Sister Mary

With Love and

GW00832414

HOARSE LAUGHS

Lewis Proops

MINERVA PRESS
LONDON
MONTREUX   LOS ANGELES   SYDNEY

ISBN 1 86106 570 1

First Published 1997 by
MINERVA PRESS
195, Knightsbridge
London SW7 1RE

Printed in Great Britain by
B.W.D. Ltd, Northolt, Middlesex

HOARSE LAUGHS

Acknowledgements

Thanks are due to my wife, Dorothy, for her patience, also to Alison and Helen for their help in typing and to John Kent for his illustrations, based on ideas of my grandson, Martin.

Contents

Introduction   9

Sergeant   13

Simon   19

Horse Hoeing   22

Cold Weather – 1942   24

Wall-Eyed Jack   27

Hedge   31

The Charge   37

Cornflakes and Golden Syrup   40

Corn Law   42

Animal Humour and Musical Mare   47

Dockside   50

Afterward   52

Introduction

To begin with, as a town boy I had never dreamed of working with horses or any other large animal. My schoolboy dreams were vaguely, of course, that I should become a famous explorer of hidden islands, or maybe a great surgeon or even a preacher – never ever a farm boy.

Born in Southampton, then the second largest passenger port in Britain, I was the second son of a police constable. My only contact with horses could have been the scrawny nag struggling to pull our greengrocer's van along the street, or a sweet little Shetland pony who appeared in the summer, pulling a dinky little ice-cream cart with bells tinkling.

In 1940 Adolf Hitler changed all that, when the roof of our house parted company with the rest of our home. It was decided that we should move swiftly to the New Forest. After several billets with cottagers, I was volunteered by my parents to work on a farm in return for a pittance, with the use of a tied cottage rent-free for as long as I remained in employment. The farmer who first employed me did not, I believe, take me very seriously. An underweight scrawny beanpole, he managed to hide me each day, putting me in the charge of his son or the aged craftsmen who guided me with patience through the simplest tasks, some out of loyalty to the 'Boss' others from compassion, which in later life I have come to value. Fortunately their tuition was based on experience gained in the years between the Great Wars. In no uncertain terms I was compelled to listen, watch and then practise. I must admit that at the start I felt most unhappy, not only with performing such menial, dirty, smelly farm tasks, but more so with the loss of personal control over my somewhat uncertain plans for my future.

As I gained experience and a modicum of confidence, life grew brighter. I felt able to parry some of the jibes thrown at me and to return as good as I got. At about this stage, I became aware that the animals I worked with were fun.

I have penned a few of the less serious incidents which consequently occurred, so read on into my light but (almost) accurate view of animal humour in the hope that you may become more aware of animal intelligence. In the future, when in the presence of a huge draught horse or stud bull at your local show ground or pageant (now probably the only likely places at which one comes into contact with such animals), observe their eyes, mouths and ears in that order. Look for a twinkle, a snigger or a twitch.

I do not profess to 'know' horses as an expert horseman should. My experiences with horses were picked up from constant association with them on the farm. Sure I knew how to hoe and plough and reap and mow as well as any by the time I was an adult, but I do feel that not enough is made of the humorous side of farm life. I suppose my zany sense of humour developed as a defence against utter boredom and the isolation of deep country living – especially when the subject was a weedy town lad, who up to 1940, had never given much thought to horses.

Sergeant, acting overworked – the chain wasn't even
connected to an implement!

Sergeant

Sergeant was an old war horse (from the 1914-18 War) – so
I was given to understand. My boss told me in confidence that
the horse (a chestnut medium draft gelding) had served with
distinction on the western front in the first great World War,
pulling in tandem great ammunition limbers across shell torn
fields in France. Yet now, twenty-three years on, the veteran
was still capable of working for a full day on the land. I also
learned that the farm situated near Romsey in Hampshire
housed an army remount, where war-tired horses were rested
and fresh new horses took over their duties. I can imagine that
Sergeant somehow changed hands at the end of the war in
payment for some service rendered to the quarter master.

In hindsight Sergeant was, I suppose, aptly named, seeing
that he had done his bit. I think he should have been named
Old Sweat or Crafty, for he knew almost every dodge there was
to avoid work, I lie, heavy work. This meant any work that he
felt was either below his dignity, or looked as if it might keep
him away from his special stall at the stable, and comfort, for
too long. Of course he would sometimes be prepared to travel

to neighbouring farms and on light haulage excursions, on the condition that he travelled at his own pace – no whips or irritating sticks – and that the reins were permitted to rest on his buttocks in a relaxed manner so that he could gauge whether any excessive call to work harder or walk faster could or would be noted and acted upon. Probably my boss Joe had conceded to the old devil over the years, because the long distance jobs usually fell to me, a callow youth who obeyed all orders from the boss as though they were God-given. Sergeant found me to be pretty transparently soft-hearted, with soft hands and no real knowledge of how an old sharpster such as him should be dealt with. So there it was: a boy, a four-wheel cart and his master, the horse. A five mile journey would be guaranteed to take over an hour. I suppose the pace triggered off the inevitable remark from Joe – " I don't suppose we'll be seeing you again before tea. You'd better have this shilling to buy yourself a bite when you get to Copythorne, and mind you don't get drunk on it!" Sniggers from the other hands also waiting around for jobs to be allocated.

A good-natured slap on the rump by Joe would upset Sergeant's equilibrium for precisely five seconds, during which he would whinny, lurch forward into the shafts and clear his bowels with great expediency. All this did nothing for my comfort, sitting high up on the box seat trying to remember which reins I should hold in which hands. I inevitably fell off the box into the cart, feet clawing at the sky, only regaining my upright position as we surged out into the gravel lane. I used to blush in those days, and embarrassment stayed with me for the first mile. I swore vengeance many times on those swines in the yard, but the responsibilities loaded onto my young shoulders soon put murder and mayhem from my mind. The main object was to keep the old horse moving in a forward direction and at an agreed pace, fast enough for progress, but not so fast as to prevent him from snatching a mouthful of sweet herb from the roadside as he passed. On this occasion I received orders to proceed to Walden's Farm to deliver four ten gallon churns of milk, in order that the lorry could pick up the two farms' milk yield and dispatch it to the railway station.

Walden's Farm, two miles away, comprised a small cluster of farm buildings and a cottage situated near the river test. The approaches to the farm were gravel tracks, one leading from the main road along a dusty path and down a one in five gradient to the buildings, the other a direct route along a level path to Romsey. The latter route was the most sought after by lorry drivers and the farmers. My route was lined by aged limes and chestnut trees; the path was bordered by lush summer grass interspersed with dandelions and herby smelling clover. The perfume that early summer morning became almost intoxicating. I drowsed as the light cart rumbled down the hill, controlled only by Sergeant's weight holding it back. The combined weight of the cart and its contents meant that I was not in control. My head lolled sleepily from side to side, completely at peace with the world, until one of nature's most devilish creations, the common horsefly or gadfly as they were locally called, managed to wreck the whole scene. The poor horse, for all his funny traits and sly demeanour, rapidly become a nervous wreck when in the presence of a 'gad'. The fly's sting (I know because I have been at the receiving end!) feels as if a fire has been lit under the skin where the sting was inserted, and the pain lasts for what seems like an eternity. As far as I know, the horse didn't get stung! He didn't wait around long enough! But gad certainly did wake him up. Once again I viewed the sky from the bottom of the cart, but this time the horse and cart were travelling full tilt down the hill. I lay wedged between two heavy churns, unable to move if I tried. The reins had left my fingers, so the old war horse fled in uncontrollable terror, seeking only to escape the tormentor. I, coward as I was, decided to stay where I had fallen. In truth I doubt whether my limbs would have responded to any mental stimulus anyway. I remember wondering if death would be quick, or slow and painful. In the ensuing race with the gad, Sergeant drove over pot holes we would have normally avoided. In doing so the lids jumped free from the churns, slopping warm milk all over me and the floor of the cart. At first I dimly imagined that I had received a mortal wound and that blood was oozing from various holes in my person.

When we arrived at the farm buildings, Sergeant decided to stop. I believe he was done in, and anyway I think the gadfly had lost interest. The farmer, hearing the racket, rushed out into the farmyard to see one very distressed young lad covered from head to foot in milk, and one very neurotic horse. The churns contained about two thirds of the milk we had started with. He quietly unloaded the churns while I unhitched the horse and sent him to a shady loose box. Then he ordered me to bathe in a concrete water trough. When my clothes dried, I returned to my boss suitably chastened, smelling evily of dried milk and endeavouring to explain to him how, although his horse hadn't exactly been stung by a gadfly, it had been a near thing, and that I hadn't really meant to drop the reins, but Sergeant had rather jerked forward when he heard the gadfly coming and anyway, although we lost a little drop of milk on the way down, we hadn't hit any gate posts, the wagon wasn't damaged and Sergeant, apart from being a little tired, did eat up all his dinner and... "Oh do shut up, you little beggar! I'm trying to work out how much your little caper cost me in milk." And that old hoss will never be the same again I'm sure. I'll have to get in the vet to give 'im the once over and who's going to foot the bill, eh? Eh! Damn all gadflies!"

Simon

Some say that opposites, when they come together, produce only good.

Well, Simon, a beautifully proportioned light chestnut three year old colt standing fifteen hands high, was the outcome of the blending of opposites; on one hand a lovable hard working mare, Flossie (of the musical fame), and on the other, Sergeant, the slowest, laziest, craftiest old war horse one could ever meet.

Simon had come of age to be broken into work (so that he could be offered for sale as a working horse). Joe, my boss, promised me (a seven stone stripling) a ride in the training cart on Simon's maiden voyage (actually he only wanted me along to act as ballast). The training cart was lightly constructed, just two wheels, shafts, sleek enough not to upset the trainee, a few floorboards and a kickboard nailed across the front of the cart to absorb the odd kick. Joe asked me to hold the colt's reins whilst he placed a pad and straps on Simon's back – even at fifteen, I could have told the boss it wasn't going to work! He made great things of a quiet approach, talking gently all the time, running his hand gently down the colt's withers, eventually placing the pad on Simon's back and miraculously fitting the girth and tightening it.

Looking very proud of his efforts, Joe then reversed Simon into the shafts of the trainer and connected him up, "So far so good," he chuckled. From where I'd been standing, close to the youngster's eyes, a different message was being relayed.

I had observed his eyes and ears. I suppose the lions at the coliseum in Roman times must have felt like Simon, just before they set upon the unsuspecting Christians; a sort of high explosive, trembling, controllable rage waiting to be released at the appropriate moment. Our 'happening' occurred just twenty yards along a leafy country lane (thank God road traffic was minimal in those days!) Simon stood on his hind legs glaring at the sky, making grand progress on two hind legs for several yards before crashing down and kicking out, punching a gaping hole in the kickboard. As I have said the cart was lightly built – so light, in fact, that the floorboards parted company, leaving just the axle, two wheels and us at the mercy of a very determined and indignant young horse. I was actually running along behind the cart when the offside wheel flew off! Joe somehow grabbed the branch of a hazel tree when the cart disintegrated. Simon came to a halt half a mile along the lane. Our elderly postmistress stood holding a quite nonchalant colt, and was in the process of giving him a peppermint when we arrived. I do not recall ever seeing Simon broken in – maybe the opposites were just too opposite.

Horse Hoeing

One of my least liked tasks, horse hoeing, entailed leading a horse up and down rows of seedlings. A horse hoe is a framework of girders bolted together in a square, a metal wheel attached to each side, two steering handles and a series of 'legs' hanging down, on the feet of which are fitted triangular and L-shaped blades. These are intended to cut through the surface of the soil, just deep enough to sever the roots of annual weeds which grow between the rows of plants. The blades are set accurately to just miss the growing plants. The person holding the handles has the difficult task of steering the blades carefully between the rows, making sure that not one of the plants is damaged, also to control the speed of forward travel and to execute clean turns at each end of the field. My small part in the proceedings was to walk beside the horse, holding its reins and trying to make sure it walked in the right row and didn't stop, or gallop across the work. Imagine, a balmy spring day, a boy, a willing horse, a sharp-tongued farmer and five acres of kale seedlings. You have already spotted the weak link, yes, after an hour in the warm sun and the intoxicating scent of mown grass my mind closed down. The reins dropped and I stumbled against the horse who, in turn, crossed four lines of plants, massacring dozens in the process. I woke to a stinging sensation as the farmer flicked the reins across my ear. A fury hitherto unknown to me welled up, tears of humiliation streamed down my face. I turned on my heel and made for the field gate. A stream of invective followed me. The horse, not having a guide, decided to come home with me. The horse hoe cut a wonderful swath through the plants, and the louder the man shouted, the faster went the horse and the contraption. When it reached me, I steadied the horse, untangled his reins and waited for my boss to catch up, expecting the very worst.

When he recovered his breath, he leaned against the gate, stared at the ground for a moment, then, looking me in the eye, said, "At least you've got pluck, young 'un. Sorry I hurt you – now let's get back to work." Mollified, I agreed. Strangely I never did horse hoe with him again, but always with someone else!

Cold Weather – 1942

The elements play a large part in farming, although each season presents farmers with elemental routines such as spring sowing, summer hay making and harvesting, autumn cleaning and winter ploughing. Variations in the weather could create huge problems. I remember, in 1942, the autumn and winter were said to be 'Russian winter weather'. A continual icy blast held half the country in its vicious grip for three whole months, delaying ploughing and putting the spring sowing back several weeks. The farm sustained a large herd of Shorthorn cows and their followers. Each beast required feeding twice daily with at least 20 lbs of foodstuff per feed.

The cold became so intense that we were forced to hold the animals within the perimeter of the farm buildings and yards, and even then the poor beasts stood around shaking with cold. Their milk production dropped quite spectacularly when the water supply froze up. Some of the herdsmen spent cold nights visiting the byres, breaking ice on the drinking troughs and seeing to it that the animals were well stocked with food.

One of my memorably painful tasks was, after milking, to go to the kale field to chop down the six foot tall plants with a machete and place them intact onto a horse-drawn trolley so that they could be hurried into the farm compound. As a not very well fed or clothed lad I dreaded the idea of kale cutting. My superiors probably imagined it would be character building for the young whelp! Within minutes of starting cutting I would be soaked through, as ice and snow splattered my clothes. The machete soon froze to my blue hands as I hacked at the stalks. The icy blast completed my discomfort. Movement became mechanical by mid-morning. The task completed and the greenstuff loaded, I would rush to the cottage door where my mother would serve me with a hot drink and a home-made bun. My swollen hands ached as the circulation returned. Mother would scold me with the threat of 'chilblains before you are much older!' Little did she know the reason for me taking the task was to ensure employment and safe tenure of the tied cottage.

On one occasion, the farmer must have relented for, as the days grew colder, the men became more reluctant to go into the fields. I was instructed to load my cart with straw bundles. Jack's feet slipped as he jolted the cart forward out of the rutted snow. Soon five men and two lads were on our way to a one hundred acre field. Our task was to remove very overgrown hedgerows and to burn the wood. The straw acted as kindling as we piled huge bushes and branches onto the glowing bonfire. Few strayed far from the warmth it provided and timber was cut and hurriedly dragged towards the heat. I am sure that day of burning saved the farm and the farmer a very unpleasant reckoning.

Wall-Eyed Jack

Jack was a piebald gelding of indeterminate age and certainly of doubtful pedigree, weighing about fifteen hundredweight when I was first introduced to him on a May morning. My new boss gestured to Jack and said, "Any experience with the big 'uns?"

I replied with alacrity that I had dealt with them before. Rather rashly, I recited how I had harrowed, cultivated, drilled and sowed at a previous establishment.

Satisfied, my new employer dismissed himself to more important business while I tried to convince myself I hadn't actually lied about my skills. What I hadn't said was that all my past experience had been gained in a few weeks one summer prior to my doing my bit for king and country, when my employers had taken me into farm work with great sympathy, virtually holding my hand through all tasks that I attempted. In modern idiom, one could say I had been talked through all the jobs. Too late now for recrimination. I needed cash – my demob gratuity was fast becoming exhausted and I

'Wall-eyed Jack'.

lived away from family and home. My landlady had demanded rent in advance, thus emptying my pockets of any spare cash. In fact I was pretty desperate to earn even the pittance farm workers received.

Jack seemed to sense my mood and gave me no trouble as I groomed him and put him into the cart harness. We were to take a load of swedes to a field nearby in preparation for a meal for the farm milking herd when they were released from their shippons. Throughout the following weeks and months, Jack and I built up a rapport – I agreed not to overload him and he agreed to keep a brisk pace going so long as the boss was in view.

Horses do possess a sense of humour – ask any of the horsey fraternity and for the price of a couple of beers or a double scotch you'll be truly surprised at the comic exploits attributed to our equine partners. Oddly, their humour (as with humans), varies from the simple naive funny, which, when it occurs, is delightfully innocent, to the sophisticated sharp wit of the satirist. Jack's humour was sometimes, I'll swear, intended to embarrass me.

My hair has always been reasonably fair, almost to the point of straw coloured, and whenever Jack decided my hair needed cutting, he would quite gently, but with firm intent, take a wisp of my hair between his lips and tug it smartly upwards. On hearing my yelp of pain, the horse would gallop away from me and after about twenty yards, he would creep back again and blow his nostrils all over me. I can assure you Jack's fun could be quite painful and eye watering.

Hedge

Jack loved a nice, long, unencumbered walk, and he really seemed to enjoy me leading him through the streets of town. At that time, our only commercial smithy plied his trade in a very aged forge situated on the side of the High Street. I suppose now the forge would be considered a listed building; its blackened beams and dangling door combined to give the little building character.

One obstacle in our little jaunts was in the nature of tram cars, well not so much tram cars as tram car drivers. Jack scorned them. He felt they were quite sub-human, especially when, on seeing him walking sedately along the footpath, they would ding their warning bells as long and as loudly and as often as possible. Jack would shake his head in attempt to avoid the noise which hurt his sensitive ears.

I suppose Jack was considered a bit of a character in the town streets, with his huge frame and black and white piebald colour, set off by his lazy left eye, which, when he travelled without his blinkers, swivelled around and peered at you with an idiotic leer. Jack, always a clown and ever inquisitive, never failed to notice details which our sophisticated vision ignored.

On one particular day in early summer, as I led Jack to the smithy I decided out of respect for the tramway company, to lead him along the pavement on the opposite side of the road. A few shops still operated, selling whatever came to hand in the way of marketing goods. The majority of the standing houses that had been spared by the Blitz and were still habitable were Victorian red-brick terrace places, each boasting a three foot wide front wall. Each had a front garden enclosed by a low brick wall, sporting neatly trimmed privet hedges, the leaves of which often became coated with soot from the dozens of chimneys venting coal smoke into the air. As we passed one such garden, an elderly man in a smart brown waistcoat prepared to trim the top leaves of his hedge. Presumably he came from a fastidious home where neatness and good visual lines were important, not only for the general appearance of the hedge, but also as a statement of the moral character of the house's occupant. He had fastened a length of string to a down pipe and had pegged the other end to a gate post. The result was a pleasingly level and straight line two inches below the top leaves of the hedge. As he progressed along the hedge with his shears, snip-snipping, the effect was a truly magnificent, level piece of work. I think even Jack was impressed, for he gave the dear man a wink from his lazy eye as we proceeded towards the smithy, and went through the rigmarole of shoeing.

Once the job was finished and Jack was feeling very proud of himself with his new shoes, the clear ringing sound of his feet pounding down on the flagstones and even producing the occasional spark as the metal struck the flint, I decided – no, Jack decided, that the return journey would take us along the same pavement that we had come down on. I led Jack from the roadside so that he could walk the pavement and avoid any hassle from grinning tram drivers. When I make mistakes I usually make big ones, as I surely did that day. I was lost in a brown study, Jack enjoying his attempts at campanology, his head held high and tail swishing. All went well with the world, until I felt a sharp tug on my left arm. There was a sound that can only be described as a swatch, followed by a shrill scream, followed by an even shriller stream of invective. I turned my head to see the cause of all this noise and saw the little man with the shears pointing upwards, purple faced, eyes wider than saucers, shouting abuse at – guess who. His efforts at topiary had been completely ruined by a huge dent in the immaculate line of hedge. Jack chewed thoughtfully on a mouthful of leaves, only seconds later realising that he didn't like privet anyway discharging them over the pavement.

A small crowd had gathered, a tramcar stopped so that the passengers could view the scene in comfort. Jack of course, loved the attention and proceeded to ogle everyone with his loose eye. As he turned to face his audience, his shoes clattered magnificently on the pavement causing people to respectfully move back a few inches. The little man became quite apoplectic as the horse turned his rear end toward him. His language became really quite threatening and his condition was not helped when one dear old lady, weighed down with a heavy shopping bag, piped up, "The wicked old sod tried to cut the horse's tail off with his shears – 'e's barmy 'e is, 'e's barmy I do declare." There was a subdued muttering from the crowd, 'poor old horse was peckish 'e only wanted a few greens.' Someone from the crowd proffered a half-eaten apple which dear Jack sucked into his big wide mouth and chewed and munched, salivating all over his bit, his loose eye rolling to the delight of the youngsters of the crowd. I felt quite heroic being the keeper of such a magnificent charge, especially as he was acting the part of victim so successfully. The little man did not leave the arena willingly. He was dragged unceremoniously through the front door by a very large woman. It was just as well really, for the excitement had affected the horses' bowels, and he deposited an enormous amount of 'rose fertiliser' in the tiny front garden and prepared to move off whilst the crowd gawped at the pile. "Lummy, what a lovely heap of manure – I'll go back for me bucket," said one.

As we swept grandly into the farmyard, my boss eyed me coldly, "You've been up to something, now, haven't you, you two!"

Cavalry charge –
'A shock wave, a gust of wind and the smell of horse sweat'.

The Charge

Jack used to play a jape called the 'organised cavalry charge'. He did this with his two stablemates, Nobby and Bet – don't ask me why a 19cwt shire gelding came to be called Bet, as feminine a name as one can imagine, yet the name was fixed and as far as I know the horse would answer to no other. The game was simple in the extreme, but very scary. Early one misty September morning, I was introduced to the charge. Not being fully awake, my eyes were not accustomed to the blurred horizon. Armed with a halter and a bowlful of crushed oats mixed with flake maize and just a touch of molasses, I clambered over the gate and ambled into the centre of the fifteen acre meadow, confidently expecting Jack's appetite to overpower his sense of discretion, thus making him an easy catch. That morning I shook the bowl and made my usual chirping noises, firmly believing I had horse language at my fingertips. A long pause, no Jack, more horse language, still no Jack. The thundering began almost imperceptibly behind my back, growing in intensity until the ground trembled. I glanced over my shoulder to see Jack, Nobby and Bet converging on me at about twenty miles per hour in perfect arrowhead formation, Bet leading. They were not fifty paces away – to run was out of the question, my feet had taken root and my limbs were paralysed with fear. I awaited the inevitable explosion of blood and bones as three tons of horseflesh collided with one hundred and forty pounds of me. The prospect was an earth shattering nightmare.

The sense of disbelief at the unfairness of fate that I should depart from this sweet life so painfully and with such ignominy to die under the hooves of my tried and trusted workmate, Jack, was too much to take in. A shock wave, a gust of wind and the smell of horse sweat – I lifted my attention to the charge. To my disbelief, I was watching the rear ends of the trio disappearing in true shell burst formation to three different sides of the field, only to see them wheeling round to look at me and, with heels high, scatter good-naturedly off to the far end of the meadow. Shock and fear drained any strength away from me, only to be replaced by a soaring bitter anger. I had been played with by these three bloody imbeciles. They had set out to, and had succeeded in humiliating me. I'll swear I heard a throaty chuckle from Jack as he made yet another near pass at me.

I felt too miserable to think clearly, so I made for the gate from which I had entered the field. Somehow I had to make up some kind of excuse to the boss as to why I was to return to the farm empty-handed while there was work to be done. The idea of persevering with the horses had not occurred to me. Beaten and very deflated, I sat on the gate with my back to the field. I was still trying to formulate a believable excuse when I felt a nudge in my back. Looking around I saw Bet behind me, towering above me with an amused twinkle in his eye. I couldn't hate that damned old fool, and I think he knew my tempers were short lived anyway. Notwithstanding, he had also spied the bowl containing the sweet smelling corn I had hoped to use as horse bait. He pressed his nose firmly into the corn, pausing only to crunch the oats and maize. I felt that Bet had sacrificed his own freedom as a form of truce, for I found no difficulty in placing the halter around him apart from a jerk of his head. He acquiesced as I led him round the field in a wide circle to show him off to the others. Inquisitiveness eventually got the better of Jack, who walked right up to me and sedately offered me his forelock. In next to no time I switched the halter onto him and, with a firm grip on him, I opened the gate and guided him through, onto the path to work.

Cornflakes and Golden Syrup

A serious fire in a local co-op warehouse ruined tons of foodstuff – meat, eggs and fish disappeared into heaps of water-soaked ash. Surprisingly, the stocks of breakfast cereal, jam and treacle escaped the signs of fire and water, but the smoke tainted them, making them unfit for retail. So, as was the practice, my boss was given the option of taking away any food suitable for pig food, on the condition that he provided transport to remove all the sludge heaped through it.

I accepted the task of moving the 'clean' food with alacrity, and at 10 a.m. on a sunny morning arrived at the site and made short work of loading piles of boxes of the most popular breakfast cereal. As I tied the load down with tarpaulin and ropes, a warehouseman threw a heavy carton of tinned jam and golden syrup onto the tailboard of my wagon. A four mile journey to the farm was pleasant, yet uneventful. On arrival I noticed that the other staff had gone to their various lunches. No horseman considers his own needs above those of his charge, so I prepared Jack, my steed, for food, and as a special treat (knowing Jack's sweet tooth) concocted a delicious menu:

cornflakes, porridge oats, a dash of Rice Crispies, liberally laced with a whole one pound tin of golden syrup. Jack needed no second bidding to the banquet. With a loud snort he buried his nose into the sticky mess. After my lunch of bread and cheese and a bottleful of cold tea, I returned to the stable to groom and prepare Jack for a further trip. I was greeted with looks from my colleagues who had already prepared their horses for work, and the farm foreman, normally a level-tempered, friendly man, glared at me from the shadows of the shed, "And what the hell do you think you are trying to do?"

I followed his eye to the dark corner in which Jack stood. The poor horse looked around on hearing my footsteps. His distress was obvious – the treacle had acted like glue and had truly fixed a thick layer of cereal over the horse's head, from the tips of his ears over his eyes and mouth, and oozing slowly down his chest to the floor. Had I not immediately rushed to the nearby trough and scrubbed Jack from head to foot, I am sure I would have received my cards and a large boot.

Corn Law

I have often been accused, quite rightly too I feel, of being heavy handed with romantic notions of animal behaviour, of seeing heavy overtones of man's love for his domestic charges, and the return of love and loyalty from them. This criticism I accept simply for the reason that I have, to date, not found a simple or undeniable boundary fence which divides fact from fantasy. The storyteller will always err on the side of romance in an attempt to draw the reader's imagination deeper into the fabric of his story. I do not, however, need soppy romance to tell of the hard men of the stable. Take, for instance, Harry, Lardy and Bonzo, yes, these were the names they answered to. They were three of the toughest men I have had the pleasure to meet. They were all in their late thirties, all horsemen – each one held a responsible position too.

Harry and his one ton shire-horse were responsible for all the local farm movements, sometimes taking a load of corn sacks to the granary, occasionally two pigs to market, or one cow to the slaughter house, perhaps a load of straw bales to the cattle yards. Harry never grew past five foot two inches and his features could only be described as shifty. His eyes were set close to his nose and his bare gum shone as he opened his mouth to speak. Harry wore a filthy beret on his head which I had never seen him without. The responsibility for the smooth-running of the farm was his, in as much as he and his steed could carry out most of the local haulage. Lardy spent most of his time in the nearby field horse hoeing, hedging, digging potatoes and working the land as far as one horse could cope.

Bonzo and his charge were on hire to the local council, and he and his massive Clydesdale stallion carried out a variety of jobs around the town streets and around the parks and public gardens. They were responsible for cleaning the stable area, grooming, mostly with curry comb and stiff brush, a daily inspection of the horses' feet, a polish of the hooves, followed by careful brushing of the 'feather', the long hairs which grow from the lower end of the horse's leg, and a special medicinal wash for any signs of lice or ticks, followed by brass or leather cleaning. That was before they started to eat breakfast! By 7.30 a.m. the horses would be roadworthy, glistening like gun metal in the early morning sunshine. After a swift appraisal by the boss, the day's instructions were issued. Each man, on receipt of his orders, would probably touch his forehead in a form of salute and lead his charge away to be set into his cart or wagon to begin his daily labours.

Harry could outswear any marine, and was never reticent in venting his spleen on whoever happened to be in receiving distance. Bad language came naturally to him, almost as a compliment to his normal speech. Nearly every other word began with a 'b' or an 'f'. Harry was so bow-legged that it was said a pig could run between his legs and not touch either of them. For all his physical deficiencies, he could hold his own against most men, and certainly against horses. To watch him lift the shafts of his huge carts, then manoeuvre his horse into reverse between the shafts was an education in itself. This complicated operation was performed without a word being spoken, just a series of clicking sounds from the side of Harry's mouth. One click brought the horse to attention, two clicks made him reverse. A different sound meant move to your left and another sound move to your right. Within seconds, the huge brute was still and standing level for Harry to lower the shafts onto the waiting pad situated in the middle of its back. He said he had never spoken human language to a horse, certainly he never praised a horse, yet they laboured together through the day as a team, each taking his part.

One day I witnessed a shocking series of events, which, at the time, seemed to me completely out of character with the farm and the people employed there. Just after the second world war, food being scarce, farmers were urged to deliver as much cereal food as was possible to the manufacturers and corn merchants. In doing so, the farm animals were only permitted a reduced amount of cereal, enough to produce energy, but certainly not enough to produce fat. Our stable contained two large wooden corn chests, each capable of containing a half a ton of loose oats or another dried cereal. At times the level of food became so low that we were literally scraping the bottom of the chests in order to find enough for our charges. The boss reluctantly ordered us to ration each horse to two small bowlfuls of oats per day, a diet to be supplemented with whatever could be spared from the vegetables grown for the dairy herd and the beef stock.

The fight was already in progress when I led my horse into the stable. Harry and Bonzo were hard at it. Fists and boots were flailing, a few decent blows were struck, although in anger the combatants had lost the accuracy of trained fighters and were mauling each other rather than hitting their targets. Bonzo, being the larger of the two, had the best weight advantage, and was beginning to do damage. Poor Harry's face had turned a brilliant yellow, blood flecks appeared from his nose and his mouth, and you could see that he was tired and hurt. Suddenly, a short handled pitch fork used for scraping straw from the stable floor appeared in his hands. His manner changed as he poked the fork at Bonzo's legs and started stabbing and jabbing at the big man's leather gaiters. Bonzo eventually submitted, standing quite still with his back to the stable door and his arms outstretched. Poor Harry trembled and shook as we took the fork away from him. Words would not come, his mouth, bitter with gall and dry with fear, failed in even his vocabulary. The fight, I learned later, was due to Bonzo accusing Harry of taking more than his ration of horse food from the bin. In hindsight, I still wonder at the men's devotion to their horses, and of the lengths they would go to to defend their rights.

Animal Humour and Musical Mare

Try to explain to a layman (or a townie as some countrymen would call them) that animals have a sense of humour, and he will smile at you disbelievingly and change the subject. In fact, many countrymen would not credit animals with this extra sense, being either too busy to notice it or not wanting to observe this wonderful phenomenon in case they should become involved.

Of course it could be said that many incidents attributed to animal behaviour are in fact the result of human clumsiness or stupidity. For instance, a jockey is dumped in the paddock in front of the gathering of race-goers – who's to say whether the horse deposited him there on purpose in a fit of high spirits, or whether the folly of an inexperienced jockey was at fault in not addressing his mount properly? I leave it to the readers to judge, but, before passing judgement, study the horse's ears: were they flat on his head, or was one forward and one back?

I once knew a musical mare who could break up any human conversation at will. Flossie could not abide long, lengthy and

Flossie of 'Musical Fame'.

detailed conversation, which is a pity because she could have learnt much, but no, after five minutes discussion, she would employ her disgusting habit of breaking wind. Flossie's anus was invariably moist, moist enough to ensure that when Flossie performed, she produced a high-pitched, fluid note similar to the tune produced on a reed whistle. Should the conversation continue, the tune would increase in volume and pitch, until there was a full-blooded orchestral descant to boot. Also, a disgusting odour would pollute the air around. People would cease talking to listen in amazement at Flossie's repertoire, forgetting altogether their petty conversation, then hurrying apart as the smell assailed their nostrils. Flossie did nothing by accident. Her refusal to involve herself in chit-chat was coldly calculated, accurately delivered and deadly effective.

Still say animals have no sense of humour?

Dockside

One of the more unpleasant tasks I ever undertook was to deliver fully grown, working horses to certain death.

In the late 1940s, after the cessation of hostilities, Britain discovered a very lucrative market on the Continent: in horse flesh. Mature horses, mostly well conditioned, although some were work-worn, were shipped across the Channel to French and Belgium butchers to be killed in what to us was a barbaric fashion, only to end up on the dinner plates of the wealthy in plush restaurants and hotels.

At the time, while employed in this trade, I felt vaguely sorry for my charges, yet naively content that we were feeding people who had not seen real red meat for five years. I had spent time in the war living among these defeated people and knew well the grim struggle they had, even to make ends meet from day to day. I fondly imagined that they would appreciate our donation of fresh meat as a change from our previous gifts of K rations and 'hard tack biscuits', valuable as they were in nourishing their families in the short term.

I often wondered if any of the beasts managed to evade the 'Net' and find work on the land. Some of them were quite capable of many years of loyal service.

Afterward

I recently attended the Annual Shire Horse Show at Peterborough Showground. The sight of over a hundred stallions, mares and foals parading round the main ring showing their prowess, and the shining wagons and carts which they towed with such ease and with such enthusiasm, gave me a tremendous boost.

The trouble was we were not permitted past the barricades to really view the beasts. With a bit of luck, I was able to visit the horse boxes and get close to some of the 'gentle giants'. Although as beautiful as they had appeared in their livery, I wondered if many of them had completed a full day's work on the land!

One came away with the impression that these horses were in reality just mannequins, walking the catwalk to earn their sponsors credit and advertising the blood lines on offer.

To me, real horsemanship is pushing your head into the flanks of 'your own horse' and grooming away the flecks of dried mud adhering to his legs and underbelly with the sure knowledge you have shared yet another day's labour with your companion and servant. It is good, though, to know that expert breeders can find the time and finance to perpetuate the various breeds of horses for use in the twenty-first century.